EARTH HAS A HEARTBEAT

BY

MAURICE MILLER

2016

TABLE OF CONTENTS

Change must happen with

The current generation

Now and not later

TRY TO SEE

The evidence of the world

Being destroyed

Day in and day out

Not something we can avoid

It's happening without a doubt

You are affected

In more ways than you know

Whether or not you accept it

Pollution continues to grow

In the air you breathe

Just because you don't see

Doesn't mean it's not there

All of this occurred

Due to lack of care

So be aware

This did not have to be

And believe it or not

The planet has been trying

To get us to see

THIS BLUE WORLD

It is all we have

But we've taken it for granted

Pushing beyond its limit

Showing us how she can't

Just stand it

No longer this way

What more can it show

Or absolutely say

Staring us all in the face

But going along with our day

As if it doesn't matter

Like we can't wait

For it to shatter

Earth's very survival

Means ours too

Stand and do more

Or watch it feel more blue

CIRCLING ACTS

Toxins in the air

And all around

Toxins wasted out

On top of the ground

And even under it

What type of thinking

Or more reasoning

Feels this is legitimate

With nothing wrong with this

The planet feels some way about it

And right is far from the word

Through all the buzz

Committing unspeakable acts

Never to be heard of

Spills in rivers and oceans

Causing such damage

And ecological commotion

Poisoning the only world we have

This is all we do

Somehow we believe

There's another world to move to

Become the solution

And make haste

Stop using the planet

To dump all of this waste

RIPPLES

The most calm and peaceful nature

Of this world

Ripple as well as

Still waters do

Ripples occurring as the after effect

Doing what nature is meant to do

But an unjust cause

Makes it stumble and fall

By the interference of man

Undoing a bond

We don't seem to understand

The flow of rivers and streams

Channeling down

Directly in between

An unusually narrow area at times

Thrashing against mighty rocks

Yet stay in line

Flowing in a vast area

In every direction

Playing a very vital part in our lives

Beyond the discretions

Of the right choice we can't decide

Each day comes and goes

With the planet withering away slowly

We never halt at anytime

But it knows

As a river flowing constantly

In the reverse direction

Running in full opposition of the time

Still waters on the rise

A situation upon every person

That can't be disguised

Impacts we can no longer hide

RIPPLE EFFECT

Scattering oil across it

And flowing downstream

Fracking deposits

Though harmless they seem

Circling toxics into the air

Moving steady upstream

In every direction

The rising sun

Shines it rays down

Attempting to push through

But blocked by heavy polluted clouds

So does the light

From the moon and stars

We're trying to fly kites

With no wind to carry us far

A spotlight on us always

Both past and present

With repeated days

Never learned one lesson

The ripples of our lives

Flows constantly

Day after day

Night after night

Regardless of time and place

Will flow nonetheless

These ripples have occurred

Having been put to the test

Until this planet can heal

We cannot afford to rest

That's if the damage is not

Beyond repair

In all of our lives

We must be aware

And start showing our world

Some love and care

Because with each ripple

We will come to know

And one day determine

The best direction to flow

THE WAVES

What if one day

The waves stop flowing

A complete standstill

Without you knowing

What if pollution was the reason?

Changing the waves

Like the coming seasons

No longer are they fun

Because their very nature

Has come undone

No more surfing

Or the rustling sound they make

As they hit the shore

The very essence of them

Is no more

Similar things are happening

To the planet

How do you feel about?

Being the bandit

GRAY EARTH

One planet

Is all we were given

Many problems arising

From all the miles driven

Look around you

And really see

The damage appearing is true

Made also by plants and factories

So much pollution around

I'm surprised the planet

Hasn't turned completely gray

Listen to the sounds

Of nature hurting every day

Our own worst enemy

That also became hers

The issues are many

In pain from what has occurred

And we continue to do

Do you actually believe or think

We have somewhere else new

To simply moved to

When this very vulnerable blue one

Will no longer do

Buckle down and change

Time to wake

And do something now

Before it becomes too late

Those that lend a hand

And become aware

United where they stand

But many more need to care

This affects us all

A global event

Rich or poor

No human is exempt

If you occupy this planet

And want to stay around

Get up and work at it

Initiate solutions found

If we can repair in time

And keep her from turning gray

Stop further damage

Leaving old habits behind

Maybe we'll get to see

The changes we made

And the planet will thank us someday

MAYDAY

The planet is in trouble

Efforts to help it heal

Needs to happen

Right now on the double

Distress is in the air

But no one seems to care

An urgent emergency

That requires our attention

Without further division

Building inventions

With better intentions

We need to get

On a roll

Before much worse events

Start to unfold

The damage around us

Is the distress signal

And the cry for help

The responsibility is clear

Not required of nothing else

Except for ourselves

Can the planet trust us?

To get what it needs

Or further delay the attention

While we watch it bleeds

IF EARTH COULD SPEAK

If the world could speak

What would it say?

Thinking will they hurt me

Again today

They are so wrong

And I'd rather be left alone

Ungrateful for my gifts

The very things they need

They wouldn't have anything

Without me

Making me sick and tired

The need to heal is dire

Injuring and draining me dry

But they need what I have

So I'm wondering why

They could do such things

I have no value to them

So it seems

I was here before them

And will be here afterwards

I wish they could leave

So I could avert

Further damage done

Before they take me to a place

That even I won't be able

To come back from

We must resolve this

For the generation now

That will precede us

COLOR CHANGE

Natural colors we see

So full of life

And very unique

But what if the carbon

We think is underneath

But in the atmosphere

Changed all of this

As it has appeared

Starts to show color

Unlike any other

Pollution takes the place

And in any case

Display colors we never wanted

With this becoming the norm

The planet always looking

Like a constant storm

No more perfect pictures

Due to unwanted issues

The planet doesn't seem alive

Not anymore

It's gone away inside

The door has closed

And no pulse resides

SHEER BEAUTY

Full of natural wonders

Both near and far

We have a beautiful planet

Our very own blue star

Breathtaking places

With majestic waterfalls

Here for the taking

Hoping to enjoy it all

Surprised it has kept

As much of its beauty

Because we have neglected

Our main duty

To protect this treasure

Doing it more harm

Through greed and selfish endeavors

Ample mountains

Oceans and streams

All the amazing beauty

That we have seen

And also shared

Our planet is unlike

Anything else

No matter where

In the universe

Time to appreciate it more

Acting as if it's cursed

Many pictures of it

In all of its glory

With each one taken

Telling a different

But memorable story

Our planet is a jewel

And very priceless

Even though most have placed

Many prices upon it

And nothing but take

Value seen out of place

So many evil deeds

That can't be erased

Treating this world

Like it can be easily replaced

It's a beautiful thing

But how long will it

Stay this way

Because it's truly dying

By the day

Enjoy this blue world

In its current form

While we still can

Before it's completely gone

CLEAR AS DAY

What's happening all around us

Is as clear as day

But we continue to act

And ignore this anyway

What will it take?

How long does the planet have to wait?

Before we move and act

On its behalf

Blocking this blue world

From further attack

Sooner or later

It will get to a point

Of no return

The damage will be greater

And nowhere to turn

When will we learn?

To appreciate this world

For what it truly is

And has always been

Killing it instead of honoring

Just continue to leave dents

What we've done

Has been no accident

CLEAN VS DIRTY

Clean air you can breathe

Dirty air you don't need

Clean water to drink

Dirty water that actually stinks

Clean power to use

Dirty power is abuse

Like lighting a fuse

Starting a blaze

But constantly breathing in

The toxic refuge

Clean is better for the planet

Being unclean is causing damage

Clean vehicles with no exhaust

Electric with no power loss

Inhaling dirty exhaust

Strong and makes you cough

Clean energy that can be sustained

Dirty energy just leaves remains

And also stains

Cleaner is better

With potential health gains

Clean is the way

Dirty has led us astray

Dirty is where we

And the planet will fall

But clean will be beneficial

To us all

GOING ELECTRIC

Being dirty has been a hit

But the planet has suffered

Because of it

Spewing out exhaust

When the answer is

And was before

Going electric

Engine sound no more

No spilling of oil

On the ground

Among other chemicals

With electric vehicles

This will not be found

Bikes are clean

And now electric versions too

Now can go even further

Than just your legs

Could take you

More range will continue

To improve

At some point in the future

Gas vehicles just won't do

We have better

So start using them too

NATURAL ENERGY

The answer we seek

Is already around us

Pay closer attention

To the gifts of nature

Than those we trust

With minds only on the monetary

Destroying the planet as we know

Forgetting that you reap what you sow

Use technology in conjunction with nature

Instead of against it

It is past time

That we realize this

Wind for power

The sun for energy

Both of these have always been

Right here to use indefinitely

Without pollution and toxicity

Cleaner is all we need to be

It will take the combined efforts

Of everyone that uses anything but

Renewable sources

Or should we allow old and dirty habits

To cause the planet to rupture

Move on this right now

With every intention

No one we can blame

If we don't rectify this and go clean

Letting greed and blatant disregard for nature

Cause our very own extinction

NO CHANCE

The planet knows the drill

Continuing to hurt it

Limiting its chances to heal

Using up resources

Like they have no end

Taking these courses

An unpopular trend

No need to be radical

To do your part

Moving slows as a turtle

To clean up its heart

And natural soul

Dirty habits have been bold

Watching the planet unfold

Into an uncertain future

That includes all living things

Destruction to this world

Is all that man seems to bring

Everyone stuck in a trance

While this world limps along

Can it be fixed in time?

Maybe no chance

THE COVER

We would need

To sound the alarm

If the planet didn't

Shield us from more harm

Protects us in ways

We still don't understand

And watches out for more

Than just humans

An ozone layer

To shield the over abundance

Of the sun's rays

Doing this unselfish act

Every single day

Certain weather

Never gets out of hand

And some events

Never approach land

Even the seas

Are kept at bay

Instead of just letting

Them run away

No hassle no fuss

Always on guard

So why don't we take it to heart

And protect her as she does for us

THE PLANET WAITS

Earth is waiting

For us to do better by her

She has grown ill

By all that has occurred

And continues each day

Being dirty is not the way

Clean is the way forward

To a better future ahead

But seems like we prefer her

Better off dead

She goes we go

What else needs to be said?

One can't do without the other

So we think

But on the brink

She will self preserve

Even if that means

Pushing all of us

Out of her way

So she may live the way

That is truly deserved

One earth is what we were given

We have made conditions here

Unhealthy for living

Stop being the cancer

Of this blue world

Instead be the cure

And start treating it

Like a rare and flawless pearl

I can just imagine

What she thinks of us

Stripping her constantly

Through greed and lust

Why would anyone ever

Destroy their own home

Winding up with nothing

Broken and all alone

Is how she feels

Us being here this way

Gave this planet a raw deal

Can we save this planet?

Hopefully if it's not too late

Start making better decisions

While the earth continues to wait

On us to help improve

And preserve what's still around

Time to build her back up

No longer can we afford

To keep tearing it down

PULSE

Feel the heartbeat

Of this world

As it pulse decreases

While being hurled

Into an unknown state

At the hands of man

Destroying this world

Little by little

Along with sacred lands

Out of tune

And no harmony

With impending doom

As the coming destiny

Listen to its cries

And open your eyes

Everything that resides here

Is out of sync

Bringing this blue world

To an uncertain brink

And just think

For just a second

Do you think it's tired

One could reckon so

We have damaged this world

More than we know

Maybe have slowed its pulse

To an absolute crawl

Not realizing its demise

Would also cause us to fall

Chaos has become the norm

Hearts and intentions gone cold

Instead of staying warm

Come to grips with this

We are running out of time

And set better acts in motion

Before the whole world flatlines

Earth is our home

Not another place like it

To call our own